ADDRESS

OF

CITIZENS OF LOUISIANA

TO THE

PEOPLE OF THE UNITED STATES.

McGill & Withrow, Printers, 1107 E street, Washington, D. C.

ADDRESS

OF

CITIZENS OF LOUISIANA,

TO THE

PEOPLE OF THE UNITED STATES.

The citizens of Louisiana have perceived with satisfaction that the people of the sister States are not unconcerned spectators of the events now transpiring within her limits, and of which it is probable no parallel can be found in the history of this or any other country. As these events were entirely brought about by the agency of officers, civil and military, of the General Government, the citizens of Louisiana, not doubting that the action of the Executive, at least, in reference to them, was the result of misapprehension of the facts, determined to adopt prompt measures for the correction of the error. At a meeting held for that purpose, representing (we may safely say) a large preponderance of the moral worth, intelligence, and wealth of the city of New Orleans, a committee of one hundred gentlemen was appointed, with instructions to proceed immediately to Washington to lay the facts before the several departments of the Government, and to solicit their aid in repairing the gross wrong which had been done and in restoring to the people the right of self-government which had been wrested from them by the most patent usurpation.

The undersigned form a part of that committee. On our arrival here we found so much misapprehension existing—even among those who are usually well informed—in regard to the origin and history of this disturbance, that we determined to publish a brief narrative of the facts.

The parties engaged in these proceedings, aware that if the facts were properly understood they would admit of no defense, now seek to belittle and conceal the question at issue, and to treat a conspiracy to overthrow the government of the State as a mere struggle for political ascendancy between Governor Warmoth and Mr. Kellogg. They allege that the former was endeavoring by some trickery or legerdemain to cheat the latter out of his election, and that the object of their proceedings was simply to frustrate this attempt. They have sedulously sought to produce the impression upon the public mind that this committee was composed of mere allies and agents of Governor Warmoth. We repel this insinuation as utterly false and unwarranted. We are not the representatives of any personal or party interest whatever. Governor Warmoth was not a candidate for any office whatsoever at the recent election, nor have we, directly or indirectly, any connection or affiliation with him. So far as his past career is concerned, there are few if any members of this committee who have not been among his most pronounced opponents; while in those measures of his administration for which he has been most loudly denounced, he had for his advisers, associates, and coadjutors, the very men who now assail him, including especially Pinchback, Antoine, Herron, and numerous others whose names figure most conspicuously in these proceedings. In reply to the other insinuations indicated above, we declare that we are no parties to and have no knowledge of any political trickery intended to defeat the true voice of the people; that we do not believe any such existed, and that we would not be here unless we could proclaim conscientiously our conviction that the men who have been foisted into the offices of the State have been not merely irregularly and unlawfully installed, but were not elected by the people, and were not and are not the choice of a majority of the voting population of Louisiana. We have not asked the Government to admit this on our simple assertion. All we have asked is that it should make a candid and impartial investigation of the facts.

With this preface, we now submit the following statement:

First. There was a general election held in Louisiana on the 4th day of November last for the election of a Governor, Lieutenant Governor, members of the General Assembly, and other State and Federal officers. At this election William Pitt Kellogg, a member of the Senate of the United States, and C. C. Antoine, Collector of the port of Shreveport, were candidates for the offices of Governor and Lieutenant Governor, and were opposed by John McEnery and Davidson B. Penn. The present Governor, Warmoth, was not a candidate for re-election.

Second. This election was conducted without riot, disturbance, or violence, and the number of votes cast was unusually large.* The returns of the election were made to the board appointed for the purpose. This board was composed, under the law, of the Governor, (Warmoth,) the Lieutenant Governor, the Secretary of State, and two other persons named in the law, viz: John Lynch and Thomas C. Anderson. The office of Secretary of State was filled at the time by Mr. F. J. Herron, who had been appointed by Governor Warmoth to fill the vacancy caused by the removal, several months before, of George E. Bovee, the legality of which removal and appointment was then in contest before the State courts. The board met, and it was resolved that Anderson and Pinchback were disqualified by reason of their being candidates for office. Warmoth then removed Herron (whom he had appointed) from the office of Secretary of State as a defaulter, and appointed and commissioned Wharton in his stead.

We have no reason to believe that the action of Governor Warmoth in the removal of Herron was based upon a desire to commit a fraud, for under the returns there was no necessity for fraud. It was prompted by his discovery of a

---

*See Appendix A and B.

plot between Herron and Lynch to falsify the returns and defeat the will of the people. This is manifest from the fact, developed in the evidence before the court, that Herron, anticipating the thwarting of his scheme, had several days before ordered a duplicate of the seal of State to be engraved, by which means he hoped to preserve the insignia of office in the event of his removal by the Governor.

Omitting further details, Warmoth and Wharton, on the one hand, assuming to be a majority of the board, and in the presence of Lynch, proceeded to elect Hatch and Da Ponte to fill the vacancies caused by the withdrawal of Pinchback and Anderson,* while Lynch and Herron afterward assembled and, under the same assumption, elected Longstreet and Hawkins. Thus there came to be two bodies—each claiming to be the returning board—one presided over by Governor Warmoth, the highest executive officer of the State and under the law the presiding officer of the board, and which had possession of all the election returns and everything necessary to ascertain the result; while the other consisted of Lynch, the removed Secretary of State, Herron, and their two appointees. Afterwards the State Supreme Court decided that the removal of Bovee and the original appointment of Herron were illegal, and Bovee was reinstated in his office. Whatever may be said of these contesting boards, it is clear that the courts of the United States had no semblance of authority to decide between their conflicting claims to office.

Third. After it had become probable that the two candidates, William Pitt Kellogg and C. C. Antoine, had been defeated, and that their opponents would be declared elected, they respectively filed bills in the circuit court of the United States for the district of Louisiana for injunction and relief. The Governor of the State, the members of the canvassing board, other citizens of the State connected with the promulgation of the returns, and certain persons elected or claiming to have been elected to the Legislature and to

---

* See Appendix C.

the Governship, were made defendants in one or other of these suits. The cause of complaint was, that they severally apprehended that they would be deprived of the offices for which they had been candidates. They claimed to have had the majority of votes at the election, and that there had been 10,000 voters prevented from voting because of their complexion and previous state of servitude, whose votes they would have received. The bill of Kellogg professed to be for the preservation and perpetuation of the evidence of the election, and to have reference to the support of a suit he might have to bring to recover the office. Antoine's suit was similar in the claims of title, and had reference in its prayers for relief to the organization of the General Assembly at the meeting called, in the proclamation of the Governor, for the 9th day of December, 1872.

Fourth. The parties to these suits were all citizens of the State of Louisiana. The object of the suits was to assert title to offices of the State in advance of any decision or announcement by any board of any person as elected, and to determine the persons to make the decision and the announcement, by the judicial authority of the Circuit Court of the United States. Pending the suits,* an *ex parte* and private order was made in the suit of Kellogg, declaring that the defendant, H. C. Warmoth, the Governor, had, in violation of the restraining order of the court, issued a proclamation and published the returns of certain persons claiming to be the board of returning officers, and proceeding as follows:

"Now, therefore, to prevent the further obstruction of the proceedings in this cause, and further to prevent the violation of the orders of this court, and the imminent danger of disturbing the public peace, it is hereby ordered that the Marshal of the United States for the district of Louisiana

* The decision of the court upon the question of jurisdiction was not rendered until 11½ o'clock on the morning of the 6th of December, whereas the order of Judge Durell, directing the marshal to take possession of the State House, was issued at a late hour of the night before, under the most peculiar circumstances, and executed before the dawn of day.

shall forthwith take possession of the building known as the Mechanics' Institute, and occupied as a State House for the assembling of the Legislature therein, in the City of New Orleans, and hold the same subject to the further order of this court, and meanwhile to prevent all unlawful assemblage therein under the guise or pretext of authority claimed by virtue of pretended canvass and returns made by said returning officers in contempt and violation of said restraining order; but the Marshal is directed to allow the ingress and egress to and from the public offices in said building of persons entitled to the same."

Fifth. The interlocutory and *ex parte* order in the suit of Antoine, the candidate for Lieutenant Governor, seems to have been made as the complement to the order above quoted in the suit of Kellogg, which directed the occupation of the State Capitol by the Marshal, with directions to prohibit what is termed in the order "an unlawful assemblage," while the same Marshal is directed to allow the ingress and egress of persons whom he might determine to be entitled to such a privilege. This order, in the case of Antoine, is comprehensive and explicit. None can mistake its import or its object. It provided:

First. That the Governor of the State be enjoined and restrained from examining the election returns or counting votes, except in the presence of officers designated in these orders, and from controlling, interfering with, or attempting to interfere with, the organization of the State Legislature, and from doing any act, or from giving any order or direction, or making any request which may directly or indirectly prevent or hinder any person from being present and taking part in the organization of the Senate on the 9th of December, or at any future day, who may be returned as a member thereof by a board composed of H. C. Warmoth, George E. Bovee, James Longstreet, Jacob Hawkins, and John Lynch, and whose name has been transmitted to Charles Merritt, Secretary of the Senate, by George E. Bovee, Secretary of State.

Second. That 20 named persons, who had been candidates for the office of Senator in the State Senate, and who were supposed to have been elected, and had been declared to be so, be enjoined and restrained from participating in any manner in the organization of the Senate, or doing any act about that organization, unless their names should appear on Bovee's list of names of members of the Senate, as transmitted to the Secretary of the Senate, Charles Merritt.

Third. About 100 persons whose names are given, and who were supposed to have been elected to the House of Representatives of the General Assembly, and had been declared to be so elected, were similarly enjoined from participating in the organization of the House of Representatives, or from doing any act or casting any vote, unless their names were on Bovee's list of members.

Fourth. The clerks of the Senate and of the House of Representatives were severally enjoined from placing on any list, or announcing, or recognizing, or designating as a member, prior to or during the organization of the respective Houses, any person whose name was not placed upon Bovee's list.

Fifth. The Secretary of State (Bovee) was enjoined from receiving any returns of the election of State officers, or of members of the General Assembly, excepting such as should be filed in his office by the board composed of Warmoth, Longstreet, Hawkins, Lynch, and Bovee.

Sixth. The Chief of the Metropolitan Police, and all of its members, numbering about 300, and the board, were enjoined from interfering with the organization of the General Assembly, and from preventing the persons on Bovee's list from entering into the halls of the Assembly.

Seventh. The persons composing the board recognized by the Governor were enjoined from acting as a canvassing board, and from declaring and publishing any calculation, statement, or proclamation of the results, or granting certificates of election, or statements tending to show any right to office growing out of ballots cast at said election.

The Marshal, assisted by a detachment from the Army of the United States, under these orders took possession of the

State Capitol, and held it on the 9th of December, when the General Assembly was to convene under the proclamation of the Governor. The egress and ingress of persons were regulated according to this order. A person named Pinchback took possession of the chair of the Senate, and directed its organization. He had been a Senator for a term that had expired. While a Senator he had been President of the Senate, and in virtue of such presidency, under the law, had acted as Lieutenant Governor after the death of Dunn, the Lieutenant Governor chosen in 1868; but at the time of these occurrences he was not merely *functus officio* as President of the Senate, but was no longer a Senator, and had no title or color of title to act as Lieutenant Governor, or to take any part in the organization of the Senate.* The House of Representatives was also organized, the U. S. Postmaster at New Orleans being its Speaker. The certificates of Bovee under the injunction were taken as conclusive evidence of membership. The House passed resolutions for the impeachment of the Governor, and thus Pinchback felt at liberty to assume the title of Governor. Two district courts were abolished, and a new court, called the Superior Court,† was established, with extraordinary powers, and, among others, exclusive jurisdiction to determine title to office, and Mr. Hawkins, one of the members of the Bovee board, which had made the election returns, was made judge. Steps having been taken by the Governor, in his official capacity, to secure a revision, by the Supreme Court of the United States, of the chancery orders of the United States Circuit Court, these bodies forthwith adopted resolutions to dismiss these proceedings.‡ The militia was placed under the command of General James Longstreet, another member of the Bovee board, and the arsenals were taken possession of by the aid of United States troops.

It has been supposed that no amount of professional energy and skill was adequate to make a *coup de main* in a chancery cause. This statement shows that a civil revo-

---

*See Appendix D. †See Appendix E. ‡See Appendix F.

lution was commenced, carried on, and accomplished within a lunar month, under the orders of a chancery court, in suits over which the court had no jurisdiction at all, whether of parties or subject-matter.* The Circuit Court of the United States is a court of limited jurisdiction, and without authority to entertain civil suits between citizens of the same State, unless the case arises directly under the Constitution and laws of the United States and jurisdiction is vested by act of Congress. Congress has no power to confer jurisdiction in any other case between such citizens. It has no authority to give jurisdiction of a suit of a citizen of the State against the State. Under the act of Congress of May 31, 1870, upon a single condition of facts, a citizen of a State may maintain a suit for an office of a State in the courts of the United States, but the State Legislature is specially excepted from the operation of this act in the same clause that excepts the office of members of Congress and Presidential electors.† The *ex parte* preliminary order in the case of Antoine is as explicit a determination of the title of the members of the Legislature, and furnishes as complete a writ of possession, as could be devised. The organization of the Legislature is effected by a simple chancery order.

Had there been resistance to the execution of these orders, and had riot and bloodshed followed, upon whom would have fallen the responsibility? By whose forbearance was it that a bloody catastrophe has not been exhibited as a scandal to the land? It sometimes happens that the executive department is tolerated, excused, or justified in acts of administration which exceed its legal powers. The arguments derived from the terms "State necessity," "public welfare," or "convenience," have here a soothing influence; but judiciary action is not entitled to any benefit from such arguments. The damage which ensues from the employment of judiciary power to accomplish other than judicial acts of administration cannot be calculated, and it is

* See Appendix G. † See Appendix H.

impossible to justify a court in determining that to be legal which is merely desirable, or that to be right which is only profitable. The order in the Kellogg case was *ex parte*. It was placed in the hands of the Marshal without notice to the parties. It proceeds for an alleged contempt by no legal procedure usual in matters of the sort, and we are not aware of any imminence of danger to the public peace which did or could justify the seizure of the State Capitol in a chancery suit between Kellogg and a canvassing board, a suit professedly brought to perpetuate testimony.

The case of Antoine displays with even more distinctness than that of Kellogg the use that has been made of judicial orders to accomplish results of which the judiciary had no cognizance. Antoine was a candidate for Lieutenant Governor, and would have been entitled to his office in January next had he been elected. With a disputed title, a month in advance, he filed this bill and obtained the order we have cited, placing under interdict the Governor, the Secretary of State, the members elect of both branches of the General Assembly, the board and all the officers and men of the police, and the members of two canvassing boards; and upon this *ex parte* order the organization of the General Assembly, at a time when he (Antoine) had no share in any of its sittings, was regulated and effected.

Since the meeting in New Orleans under which the committee was appointed, we have been met with the suggestion that these orders and acts are facts accomplished, and that their revocation or rescission would not restore the *status quo*, and that our complaints, therefore, are unreasonable. If the opinion we have be correct, such a circumstance ought not to affect our action or conduct. When the King of Great Britain established arbitrarily a government in one of the colonies, the remaining colonies took the alarm, lest it might serve as a precedent as well as an instrument to establish such governments elsewhere. Besides, men are less patient under wrongful orders and acts of a judiciary tribunal than even of violence from other sources of authority. A government which rests for its organization upon an illegal judicial order, executed by a marshal with companies of soldiers, does not command as much respect or authority as if the judicial appendages had been dispensed with, and the army had set up the government with a strong and usurping hand.

The committee take the liberty to say that they have had no connection with these suits as parties or attorneys; neither do they claim any of the offices in dispute. They have not heretofore been concerned in the controversies among the political classes which have endangered the peace of, and brought scandal upon, the State. They affirm that, during the last four years, there has not been good government in Louisiana. There has been extravagance, prodigality, dishonesty, and waste in the public expenditures. The public debt has been enormously increased, with but little corresponding benefit. The credit of the State has been given to speculating corporations, for personal aims. The taxes on property have assumed such proportions that they might appropriately be called rents paid by the proprietors to the State for its occupation and use. The taxes upon business oppress the commercial and laboring classes. The laws to control elections, corporations, and public institutions stimulate these excesses of office-holders, and the consequence is universal depression and discontent. The State needs an honest, faithful, and responsible government, conducted to attain public objects, and not to enrich its members or to perpetuate their power. There was an earnest effort to obtain such a government at the last election, but a political conspiracy has unfortunately defeated it.

We affirm, without fear of contradiction, that the foregoing statement exhibits on the part of the United States court the most high-handed usurpation of jurisdiction and authority of which the annals of jurisprudence afford any example.* The action of the returning board recognized and vested with all its powers by this court, has been

---

* See Appendix I.

equally unprecedented. Without any official returns before them, without any of the official data on which alone their action could have been rightfully based, they have presumed to proclaim the results of the election. The declaration by them of the votes cast in the different parishes is as purely fanciful as if no election whatever had been held.

The have arbitrarily reduced and increased the votes on one side or the other in different parishes to suit their purposes. In several parishes, while retaining or even adding to the votes cast for their candidates, they have simply annihilated or stricken out entirely the votes cast for their opponents. In other parishes they have exactly reversed the returns, giving to their candidates the majority which had really been returned for their opponents.* They have not pretended to furnish the public with any explanation of the basis on which they proceeded, or the theory on which they acted. Their whole conduct is without any kind of reasonable explanation.

We submit to the people of the United States that such proceedings reach a point at which the whole theory of popular government is reversed and overthrown. The means by which such results have been reached are enough to startle the public mind, but the results themselves are not less appalling. Aside from the general offices of the State, we find the Legislature of the State delivered over into the hands of men who were not elected, and who are utterly unfit for positions of such responsibility. As originally composed at its organization, it comprised sixty-eight persons of color, most of them totally uneducated, with a very small minority of whites. Since that time they have expelled members whose seats were uncontested. They have unseated conservative members returned elected by their own board, and seated their defeated opponents, on the simple ground that the former had not appeared to claim their seats.† The result is that, originally bad as the Legislature was, it makes itself worse day by day, and the

---

*See Appendix J. †See Appendix K.

prospect is that soon the conservative element of the State will have no representation whatever. To those who flattered themselves with the hope that Mr. Kellogg would not willingly abet any scheme of outrageous misgovernment, it is now apparent that, even supposing this to be true, the power of restraint has passed entirely beyond his control, and that, should he attempt to thwart the schemes of this Legislature, his own impeachment would be a probable event of the future.

In conclusion, we would state that we have attempted to perform the duties of our mission in the purest non-partisan spirit, and that we have not sought to furnish capital to any political party or to excite popular clamor in the interests of any faction. We have laid our case before the President and his Attorney General, and we willingly testify that we have been courteously received and patiently listened to. While they have refused the specific measures of relief for which we applied, they have given reasons for such refusal in no manner implying any indisposition to see justice done.

They have referred us to Congress, and we feel assured that we shall have the immediate sanction of the President so far as we invite an impartial investigation of the facts of our case, and that we shall have his co-operation in any measures of relief which Congress may adopt after such investigation. The people of Louisiana, ignoring party, are conscious of having made an honorable effort to place in office men of tried probity. They seek justice, not generosity. They ask for a calm, impartial examination into the recent extraordinary occurrences within their borders, in order that the truth may be known, and that there may be a speedy correction of the dangerous evils now threatening the very life of their State.

WASHINGTON, D. C., *Dec.* 23, 1872.

J. A. Campbell,	John Fairbanks,
J. Aldigé,	C. E. Fenner,
August Bohn,	E. B. Wheelock,
Joseph Bowling,	A. B. Griswold,

N. Barnett,
A. Chiapella,
J. S. Copes,
H. W. Conner,
H. D. Coleman,
John C. Potts,
John F. Pollock,
J. Tuyès,
James Wallace,
Walker Fearn,
D. C. Labatt,
H. O. Seixas,
J. W. Labouisse,
D. West,
Richard Taylor,
Mayer Stern,
R. Pugh,
George W. Squires,
G. Kohn,
H. McCloskey,
G. W. Nott,
H. V. Ogden,
W. S. Pike,
F. A. Haber,
H. Gardes,
P. M. Baker,
Albert C. Janin,
S. Hernsheim,
T. H. Kennedy,
J. M. Scott,
Al. Miltenberger.
H. G. Darcy,
Sella Martin,
W. Marks,
C. M. Wilcox,
H. R. Cramer.

APPENDIX.

A.

The New Orleans *Republican,* (the organ of the Radical Republican party,) of the 19th of November, in an editorial article, admitted frankly and unequivocally that the election held on the 4th of that month was the fairest and most peaceable ever known in the State of Louisiana; that no negro had been deprived of his right to vote because of his color; that there had been every disposition to allow to him the unmolested enjoyment of his rights; and that complete conciliation existed between the two races.

B.

The total vote in November last for Governor, exclusive of the three parishes of St. James, Terrebonne, and St. Tammany, from which irregular and informal returns only were received, amounted to 128,402. The total vote of the State in 1870 was only 106,542.

C.

Extract from New Orleans evening papers of November 13*th.*

When the board met to-day, Governor Warmoth, Acting Secretary of State Herron, and Senator John Lynch being present, the Governor, after the reading of the minutes, presented the certificate of Auditor Graham, to the effect that, Secretary of State Herron being a defaulter, he had been compelled by the constitution and laws to suspend him from the exercise of his functions, on charges which would be enumerated to the Senate. Accordingly Secretary of State Herron was requested to withdraw from the board, which he did. The Governor next presented the commission, and the evidence of his qualification for the office, of Colonel J. Wharton, as the successor of General Herron. Colonel Wharton was in the ante-room, and on being sent for promptly appeared and took his seat in the board.

Governor Warmoth then proposed the name of F. H. Hatch as a substitute for Lieutenant Governor Pinchback, which was adopted by the votes of Governor Warmoth and

Secretary of State Wharton, Senator Lynch voting "No." It was further moved that Durant Daponte be elected in place of Senator Thomas Anderson. These nominations were adopted by the board, whereupon Senator Lynch retired. The board, being thus completed according to law, will proceed to its duties.

D.

On Monday, November 9th, at the Mechanics' Institute, at the organization of the Senate, pursuant to the Governor's proclamation, it was desired by a majority of the holding-over Senators, and which majority were nearly all Republicans, that the names of those holding over, and of those returned by both boards, should first be called. These Senators, according to all law and precedent, would then determine who were entitled to seats in all cases of doubt or where no returns had been made by the Custom-house board. But this did not suit the purposes of the Custom-house party. Mr. Pinchback, who had called the Senate to order, refused to recognize any motion whatsoever, and ordered the calling of the roll according to the list prepared at the Custom-house. General McMillen, a staunch Republican, sprang to his feet, and objected to the arbitrary ruling and usurpation of Mr. Pinchback. The latter refused to hear him or to receive his protest. Other Republicans, General H. J. Campbell among the number, denounced Mr. Pinchback's action, and protested against his presiding over the Senate. Their efforts were useless. United States marshals and United States soldiers were on every hand, and their instructions from E. H. Durell, judge of the United States district court, were to obey the behests of Mr. Pinchback.

And this is the reason why objections were made to Mr. Pinchback's further presiding over the Senate. He was elected in 1868 Senator from the second district of New Orleans for a term of four years, which expired at the last election, when ex-Lieutenant Governor A. Voorhies was elected to succeed him. At the death of Lieutenant Governor Dunn, Senator Pinchback was elected President of the Senate, and thereby became Lieutenant Governor *ex officio.* At the regular session of 1872 Mr. Pinchback *always claimed the right to vote as Senator, and did so vote*, as the journal will show.

When ex-Governor M. Hahn resigned his office, and J. Madison Wells, Lieutenant Governor, became Governor in his stead, Senator Louis Gastinel was chosen President of the Senate, and thereby became *ex officio* Lieutenant Governor. All acts thereafter passed during that term are signed "Louis Gastinel, *ex officio* Lieutenant Governor and President of the Senate." That was according to the law of 1865, which says that, when a vacancy shall occur in the office of Lieutenant Governor, "the Senate shall elect a President, who shall be Lieutenant Governor." This law has been copied verbatim in Ray's Revised Statutes, 1870. At the ensuing election Governor Wells was a candidate for re-election, and Judge A. Voorhies for Lieutenant Governor. Immediately after the election Governor Wells called a special session of the Legislature, to assemble at Mechanics' Institute, November 25, 1865. The Senate having been called to order by the President, Mr. Gastinel, Mr. Kenner objected to his presiding any further, as his term of office had expired, and his successor was present. Thereupon Mr. Victor Burthe, of Jefferson, was placed in the chair as President. On the 2d of December the votes for Governor and Lieutenant Governor were counted, and on the 4th Mr. Albert Voorhies was installed as Lieutenant Governor, thereby becoming President of the Senate.

There is a precedent: the case is precisely in point; the facts agree in every respect. The Senate is the sole judge of the qualifications of its members, and it has given a construction to a law which has been re-enacted since that construction of it. Judge Durell is without authority, even under the enforcement law, to create a Legislature or in any way control its organization. It is deemed proper that these facts and this precedent be spread abroad through every State, and the National Government be fully apprized that the man who has been recognized as "Acting Governor of Louisiana" is absolutely without right to hold such office.

E.

An Act to establish an additional district court for the parish of Orleans; to define and limit the jurisdiction, and to determine the powers thereof; to provide for the transfer of certain cases now depending before certain other district courts for said parish to the court hereby created; to authorize the Governor to appoint a judge and a clerk for said court, and to provide a court room for said court; to abolish the Seventh and Eighth District Courts for the parish of Orleans, and to provide for the transfer of the records and suits in said Seventh and Eighth District Courts to other courts in said parish.

Section 1. *Be it enacted by the Senate and House of Representatives of the State of Louisiana in General Assembly con-*

vened, That there shall be, and is hereby established, an additional district court for the parish of Orleans, which shall be known and designated as the Superior District Court for the parish of Orleans.

SEC. 2. *Be it further enacted, etc.*, That the Superior District Court hereby created shall have *exclusive* jurisdiction in and for the parish of Orleans, to issue writs of injunctions, mandamuses, quo warranto, and to entertain all proceedings, and to try all cases or actions in which the right to any office, State, parish, or municipal, is in any way involved. * * * * * *

SEC. 6. *Be it further enacted, etc.*, That the offices of judge and clerk of the Superior District Court for the parish of Orleans, hereby established and organized, shall be deemed to be vacant as in case of original vacancy. The Governor shall at once fill such vacancies by appointment.

* * * * * * *

SEC. 7. *Be it further enacted, etc.*, That the act of the General Assembly, approved March 16, 1870, entitied "An act to establish an additional district court for the parish of Orleans, to define the jurisdiction thereof, and to reorganize and determine the jurisdiction of the existing seven district courts for the parish of Orleans," be and the same is hereby repealed, in so far as it establishes and organizes the Eighth District Court for the parish of Orleans; it being the intent and purpose of this act to abolish the said Eighth District Court for the parish of Orleans, and the said Eighth District Court for the parish of Orleans be and is hereby abolished. * * * * * *

SEC. 8. *Be it further enacted, etc.*, That the Seventh District Court for the parish of Orleans be and is hereby abolished. * * * * * *

SEC. 9. *Be it further enacted, etc.*, That all laws or parts of laws in conflict with this act be and the same are hereby repealed, so far as they are in conflict, and this act shall have force and effect from and after its passage.

(Signed) CHARLES W. LOWELL,
Speaker of the House of Representatives.

(Signed) A. B. HARRIS,
President of the Senate and Acting Lieutenant Governor.

Approved December 11, 1872.

(Signed) P. B. S. PINCHBACK,
Lieutenant Governor and Acting Governor of Louisiana.

A true copy:
GEO. E. BOVEE,
Secretary of State.

F.

An Act relative to the office of Attorney General, and directing the discontinuance of certain proceedings before the Supreme Court of the United States.

Section 1. *Be it enacted by the Senate and House of Representatives of the State of Louisiana in General Assembly convened:* Whereas the Hon. A. P. Field has been duly promulgated as having been elected to the office of Attorney General of this State; * * * * * * and whereas other persons are claiming to represent the State of Louisiana in judicial proceedings: That the said A. P. Field, and his legal successors, and those acting under him or them, be alone authorized to institute or continue in the name of the State of Louisiana any suit or judicial proceeding, and all other persons are prohibited from doing the same.

* * * * * * *

Sec. 2. *Be it further enacted, etc.*, That the said A. P. Field is authorized and instructed to discontinue any and all proceedings instituted in the Supreme Court of the United States by H. N. Ogden or any other person in the name of the said State.

Sec. 3. *Be it further enacted, etc.*, That this act shall take effect from and after its passage.

(Signed) Charles W. Lowell,
Speaker of the House of Representatives.

(Signed) A. B. Harris,
President of the Senate, Acting Lieutenant Governor.

Approved December 10, 1872.

(Signed) P. B. S. Pinchback,
Lieutenant Governor, Acting Governor of the State of Louisiana.

A true copy:
George E. Bovee,
Secretary of State.

G.

Constitution of the State of Louisiana.

Art. 52. No member of Congress or any person holding office under the United States Government shall be eligible to the office of Governor or Lieutenant Governor.

ART. 4, SEC. 21. No person holding any lucrative office under the United States, or any other Power, shall be eligible to any civil office of profit under this State.

CASE.

Searcy v. *Grow*, (15 California Reports, 117):

The court, consisting of Chief Justice Stephen J. Field, and Associate Justices Baldwin and Cope, say:

"The counsel for the appellant contends that the true meaning of the constitution is, that the person holding the federal office described in the 21st section is forbidden to take a civil State office while so holding the other; but that he is capable of receiving votes cast for him, so as to give him a right to take the State office upon or after resigning the federal office. But we think the plain meaning of the words quoted is the opposite of this construction. The language is not that a federal officer shall not *hold* a State office while he is such federal officer, but that he shall not, while in such federal office, be *eligible* to the State office. We understand the word 'eligible' to mean capable of being chosen—the subject of selection or choice. The people in this case were clothed with this power of choice; their selection of the candidate gave him all the claim to the office which he has; his title to the office comes from *their* designation of him as sheriff. But they could not designate or choose a man not eligible, *i. e.*, not capable of being selected. They might select any man they chose, subject only to this exception, that the man they selected was capable of taking what they had the power to give. We do not see how the fact that he became capable of taking the office after they had exhausted their power can avail the appellant. If he was not eligible at the time the votes were cast for him, the election failed. We do not see how it can be argued, that by the act of the candidate the votes which, when cast, were ineffectual, because not given for a qualified candidate, became effectual to elect him to office. Can it be contended, that if Grow had not been a citizen of the county or of the State at the time of the election, or had been an alien at that time, that the bare fact that he did so become a citizen at the time he qualified would entitle him to the office? Or suppose a man, when elected, under sentence and conviction for crime—if such a case can be supposed—would a pardon before qualification give him a right to hold the office? When the words of the constitution are plain, we cannot go into curious speculation of the policy they meant to declare. It may, however, have been a part of the policy of the provision quoted to prevent the employment of federal patronage in a State election."

H.

Act of May 31, 1870.

SEC. 23. *And be it further enacted*, That whenever any person shall be defeated or deprived of his election to any office, *except elector of President or Vice President, Representative or Delegate in Congress, or member of a State Legislature*, by reason of the denial to any citizen or citizens who shall offer to vote of the right to vote on account of race, color, or previous condition of servitude, his right to hold and enjoy such office, and the emoluments thereof, shall not be impaired by such denial; and such person may bring any appropriate suit or proceeding to recover possession of such office; and in cases where it shall appear that the sole question touching the title to such office arises out of the denial of the right to vote to citizens who so offered to vote on account of race, color, or previous condition of servitude, such suit or proceeding may be instituted in the circuit or district court of the United States of the circuit or district in which such person resides. And said circuit or district court shall have, concurrently with the State courts, jurisdiction thereof, so far as to determine the rights of the parties to such office by reason of the denial of the right guaranteed by the fifteenth article of amendment to the Constitution of the United States, and secured by this act. (Stat. at Large, Vol. XVI, p. 146.)

I.

By the decree or, rather, the interlocutory order of a United States district judge, it is attempted, in spite of the overwhelming expression of the will of the people of the State, to establish over the State of Louisiana a government consisting of a United States Senator for Governor, the Collector of a Port as the Lieutenant Governor, the United States Treasurer for State Auditor, a Surveyor of the Port for

President of the Senate, the Postmaster of New Orleans for Speaker of the House, a Deputy Collector for Chairman of the Finance Committee of the Legislature, and a Legislature composed principally of defeated candidates, most of whom are in the employ and pay of the Federal Government.

J.

Extract from the Message of the Governor, of December 11, 1872.

It is scarcely necessary to state what is so well-known to all of you, that the election recently held was fairly and honestly conducted under the laws of the State, and that the registration and the vote were both unusally full, the latter being the largest ever cast in Louisiana.

The total vote for Governor, exclusive of the three parishes of St. James, Terrebonne, and St. Tammany, from which irregular and informal returns were received, amounted to 128,402, an increase of 21,860 on the vote of 1870. The Republican vote, estimating and adding the three omitted parishes at the same vote cast in 1870 (3,734,) is only 2,461 below the vote cast for the Republican State ticket at the last election, and it is well known that thousands of Republican voters throughout the State, at this election, supported the Fusion ticket. The returns made by the State officers were in due form, and these returns are the only official evidence in existence of the vote at the late election. The pretense of the agents selected by Senator Kellogg to promulgate an official falsification of the result, that they have made a compilation of the votes, is only one of the bold and audacious falsehoods by which every step of the conspirators has been marked. Those persons had no returns, no documents, no evidence of any kind in their possession, except the statements made up by themselves and their allies for the consummation of their fraudulent purposes. A comparison of the tabulated statement published by them with the genuine returns, as previously published, shows that they did their work in flagrant defiance of decency, and without even an attempt to conceal their fraud and falsehood from the eyes of the public. The bill filed by Senator Kellogg alleged simply a deficiency in his returned vote of about 10,000, due to an alleged suppression of a portion of votes actually cast and a refusal to register or to receive another portion. The alleged suppression was totally false, and was supported by no evidence whatever—not even the simulated cross-mark affidavits with which the conspirators so liberally provided themselves in advance. The affidavits filed by them amounted to about 4,000 in number, according to their own statement. If they had simply added this number to the total, it would have given Senator Kellogg 64,233 votes, against 68,169 for McEnery, not enough to show an apparent election, even including the vote for the three omitted parishes. They therefore, without returns, without testimony of any kind, without even adopting and following any rational theory of computation, added the enormous number of 12,675 to Senator Kellogg's vote, and as if to still further insult the intelligence of the public, and still more flagrantly expose their own falsehood and wickedness, they deliberately struck off 14,140 from the vote cast for Mr. McEnery. The returns from the parish of Bossier were, for McEnery 953, for Kellogg 555. They report for Kellogg 1,159, for McEnery none. The vote of Natchitoches was for McEnery 1,250, for Kellogg 550. They report for Kellogg 1,206, for McEnery none. In Assumption they have added 504 to Kellogg's vote, and subtracted 454 from McEnery. In Avoyelles they add 525 to Kellogg's vote, and subtract 454 from McEnery's. In East Baton Rouge they add 1,343 to Kellogg's vote, and subtract 727 from McEnery's. In De Soto they add 578 to Kellogg's vote, and subtract 660 from McEnery's; in Plaquemine they add 1,129 to Kellogg's vote; in St. Landry they add 545 to Kellogg's vote, and subtract 555 from McEnery's; in Vernon, where McEnery has 669 votes, they allow him 112; in Winn, where McEnery has 575 votes, they allow him 127; in Washington, where McEnery has 453 votes, they allow him 194; in St. Mary they add 300 to Kellogg's vote, and subtract 500 from McEnery's; in Union, where McEnery has 1,418 votes, they allow him 460; in Orleans they strike between 3,000 and 4,000 from McEnery's vote; and in almost every parish they have made changes equally capricious and irrational, and returns equally false and fraudulent; and these are the men who based their suit at law upon the charge that the Governor and the returning officers intended to falsify, to mutilate, and to destroy the election returns. These returns are in existence; they retain all the integrity of their original form. They are unmutilated and unfalsified; they constitute the only evidence of the late election that any law recognizes, or that any honest judicial tribunal would accept. They have never been in the hands of the conspirators, and yet these persons, pretending to act as public officials, have promulgated results so monstrously at variance with the truth, that they seem to court the notoriety of falsehood and to revel in the publicity of fraud.

K.

Extract from a report of the proceedings of the Legislature.

"HOUSE.—The House met at 12 m. Seventy members present. Mr. Sauer in the chair.

Mr. Demas introduced the following resolution, which was adopted:

Whereas the Committee on Elections and Qualifications of this House have, after due investigation, reported favorably upon the applications of W. H. Decker and Radford R. Davis, Representatives from the Tenth Representative District, parish of Orleans;

Whereas the said W. H. Decker and Radford R. Davis are the only applicants for seats as Representatives elect to this House;

And whereas the people of the Tenth and Eleventh Wards of the parish of Orleans, comprising the said Tenth Representative District, are now without representation or voice in the Legislature of this State:

Resolved, That in consonance with the report of the Committee on Elections of this House, and in view of the fact that the said Decker and Davis are the only applicants for seats in this body, that the said Decker and Davis be and they are hereby admitted to seats in this House, subject to any contest which may be hereafter made."

The members elect denied seats by this resolution are Messrs. James McConnell and James B. Eustis, who were elected by overwhelming majorities, and whose election was admitted by the Custom-house board, but who absented themselves from the Legislature because of the illegality of its proceedings.

The same action was taken by the Senate in reference to Messrs. McMillen and Campbell.

How the right to seats in the Legislature is determined.

The following resolution, offered by Mr. Bryant, of East Baton Rouge, was also adopted:

"Whereas the legal returning board, composed of Messrs. Lynch, Longstreet, Bovee, and Hawkins, have carefully examined, counted, and officially promulgated the election returns of members of the House of Representatives, elected at a general election held on the 4th day of November, 1872: therefore, be it

Resolved, That the members so returned are hereby confirmed as the legal members of the House of Representatives of the State of Louisiana."

To the People of the North.

New Orleans, *Dec.* 13, 1872.

The undersigned representatives of houses in the North doing business with the South, who have been visiting New Orleans for many years past and at present, and are thoroughly conversant with the political feelings of the people of this section, wish to express our opinion at this critical juncture of affairs.

Visiting New Orleans at a season when the city is usually full of activity and life, we find every channel of trade paralyzed, the State House occupied by troops, the officers of the State threatened and intimidated, and the people cast into the deepest gloom by the arbitrary usurpation of power and place by political adventurers, backed by a United States judge, who has called in the assistance of United States troops to execute his decrees.

After an election, which we believe to have been conducted as fairly and honestly as any in which the American people ever participated, finding themselves beaten by a large majority of the votes of the citizens of this city and State, this unscrupulous and irresponsible body of men have resorted to trickery and violence to defeat the execution of the will of the people as thus expressed.

Believing this action the greatest outrage every attempted to be carried out in our country, and one which tends directly to the overthrow of the liberties of the people, and to destroying the power and sacredness of the ballot-box, we hereby enter our solemn protest against the high-handed action, and appeal to our fellow-citizens of the North to unite in protesting to Congress and the President, to the end that the legally elected officers of the State may be installed in office, and the people of the community supported in their efforts to exercise the right of franchise, that they may redeem their State from the bankruptcy and ruin with which it is now threatened through the action of these nameless adventurers.

Charles A. Griffith, representing A. D. Hopping &

Wilson, 218 and 220 Washington street, New York.

John D. Dargen, John G. McMurray & Co., 277 Pearl street, New York.

George Lipsher, W. W. Eastham, 129 Broad street, Boston.

Thos. S. Darling, Detroit Watch Works, Detroit, Mich.

E. P. Briggs, H. & J. W. King, 80 Chambers street, New York.

William C. Ilsley, Ilsley & Co., 254 Pearl street, New York.

W. S. Ridgway, J. W. Gaff & Co., 11 Pub. Landing, Cincinnati, Ohio.

John W. Poole, Wm. R. Warner & Co., 154 North Third street, Philadelphia.

J. H. Hapgood, New York Brush Company, 254 Pearl street, New York

Amos Patten, W. K. Lewis & Bros., 93 Broad street, Boston.

George D. Strong, La Belle Glass Company, Bridgeport, Ohio.

E. N. Belt, of Cahn, Belt & Co., 32 West Lombard street, Baltimore.

W. R. Bennett, Tilden & Co., New York.

B. F. Lieber, B. Lieber & Son, 111 and 113 South Water street, Philadelphia.

E. H. Packer, Whittemore Bros., 579 Broadway, New York.

E. H. Packer, Bachelore, Moore & Co., Boston.

E. H. Packer, M. & H. Shrienkheim, New York.

E. H. Packer, Corry & Hooper, Boston.

E. H. Packer, Bedford Chain Company, New York.

Alexander Torges, Jr., L. A. Strobel & Bros., Cincinnati, Ohio.

A. Flesh, A. & D. Flesh & Co., Frankfort, Germany, and 351 Broadway, New York.

W. G. Morse, New York city.

C. E. Knapp, D. P. Ketehum, New York city.

Frank Hegger, E. H. Van Ingen & Co., New York city.

Douglas H. Duer, John Duer & Son, 24 South Charles street, Baltimore.

William C. Mudge, H. B. Mudge, 95 West Second street, Cincinnati.

E. C. Coolidge, John K. Coolidge & Co., 244 West Second street, Cincinnati.

Ed. V. Bermingham, John McKittrick & Co., 522 North Main street, St. Louis.
Edmund J. Godine, Wright Bros. & Co., 324 Broadway, New York.
Gustave A. Jahn, Frederick Lyman & Co., 90 Wall street, New York.
W. C. Simmons, Jr., Providence, R. I.
E. Maitland, T. W. Devoe & Co., 115 and 117 Fulton street New York.
A. Rutzer, Linseed Oil Company, 235 Pearl street, New York.
D. Hirsch, of Hirsch & Co., 174 Water street, New York.
Joe Harrison, Royal Chemical Company, 191 Duane street, New York.
J. T. Burdeau, agent Mississippi Valley Transportation Company, St. Louis, Mo.
R. E. Parker, agent McKesson & Robbins, 91 Fulton street, New York.
T. Simmons, agent Joseph Schrœder & Co., Balimore, Md.
John Butler, Austin Thorp & Co., New York.
Albert Ingard, Rubber Clothing Company, New York, Chicago, St. Louis, and San Francisco.
John Butler, Jr., John Thompson & Co., New York.
Patrick J. McPhillips, W. H. Horstmann & Sons, New York, Philadelphia, and Paris, France.
J. G. Case, General Superintendent Champion Cotton Gin Company, 102 State street, Boston, Mass.
J. B. Goldstein, H. Block & Co., 23 and 25 East Second street, Cincinnati.
J. J. H. Hill, Bodenheim, Meyer & Co., 149 Duane and 9 Thomas street, New York.
Henry M. Woolf, Willard Felt & Co., New York.
George Felthouse, same, Cincinnati.
J. T. Sanford, Giles, Grales & Co., 13 Maiden Lane, New York.
John G. Irish, Charles Lippincott & Co., 914 and 916 Filbert street, Philadelphia.
S. Y. D. Arrowsmith, Buckenham, Cole & Hall, 10 Maiden Lane, New York.
J. P. Todd, firm of W. S. De Van & Co., Cincinnati, Ohio.
Nath. P. Snelling, Pearson Bros. & Co., Boston.
Alex. Lamby, Paton & Co., New York.

J. W. Blake, of Hall & Blake, 20 Courtlandt street, New York.
U. F. Wilcox, John S. Dunham, 117 North Sixth st., St. Louis, Mo.
Samuel Friedman, 40 Maiden Lane, New York.
Charles Lee, Charles Lee, Boston, Mass.
D. Davies, of A. M. & R. Davies, 508 Broadway, New York.
L. Wilkins, A. Henderson, 82 Water street, New York.
F. C. Rogers, of H. A. Rogers & Co., 50 and 52 John street, New York.
W. N. Johnson, of Mills, Johnson & Co , Cincinnati.
Walter Lyon, St. Louis, Mo.

Editorial article of the New York Herald, of December 26, 1872.

IS THIS A REPUBLIC, AND IS LOUISIANA ONE OF THE UNITED STATES?—Either this is a republic or it is not. Either the States manage their own local affairs or they do not. Whatever appearances may denote, we believe we are not rash in assuming that the people of the United States do live in a republic; further, we boldly quote the Constitution and decisions of the Supreme Court to prove it incumbent upon the United States "to guarantee to every State in the Union a republican form of government." In other words, every State is a republic within a republic. Now, as our creed in the late civil war affirmed secession to be unlawful, as we proved the right by our might on the battle-field, Louisiana is in the Union, because she never was out of it, and is entitled to a republican form of government, because she is a State. Hence it follows that the imperial policy being pursued towards her is an unwarrantable insult to a conquered, law-abiding, free (?) people. Ignorance is a two-edged sword. Negroes demoralized by designing leaders are no better than low whites demoralized; and what if a legislature like that of Louisiana should become uncontrollable? Already its members are loud in their threats against their defeated opponents. May it not be possible for them to turn upon their white instigators? We say this not because negroes are black, but because these particular negroes are from necessity totally uneducated, and have been played upon ever since they had political power.

Undoubtedly it was a mistake in the Liberal Republicans of Louisiana to dally with Warmoth in the late election. * * * * In spite of their aversion they accepted his aid; but his is the power of the boomerang, and returns to delay, if not to destroy, reform. Few of the New Orleans committee but were his fierce opponents in the past, yet the administration organ in this city intimates that they are "really acting in the interest of Warmoth." And what do this committee ask—a committee representing such vital interests as to draw around them thousands of citizens to wish them "Godspeed" when, in a drizzling rain, they depart for Washington? What do they ask? Anything unreasonable? Why, their story is twice told, and yet we shall repeat it again and again, in the hope of bringing the North to its senses and Congress to its duty.

They ask the Federal Government to make a candid and impartial investigation of the facts we have so often put before our readers. They maintain, and we have every reason to believe them, that they have not heretofore been concerned in the controversies among the political classes which have endangered the peace and brought scandal upon the State. They picture two distinct governments claiming sovereign jurisdiction, the United States and State courts in direct conflict, Judge Durell, under color of the enforcement act, overturning the entire State administration with one hand, while he seizes an opposition newspaper with the other, plotting, we are told, for a nomination to the federal Senate. No wonder that strong men weep; no wonder that commercial travelers in New Orleans, representing more than thirty New York houses, address a memorial to the people of the North, protesting against the "arbitrary usurpation of power and place by political adventurers, backed by a United States judge, who has called in the assistance of United States troops to execute his decrees!"

It was not treason that the Liberal Republican Governor-elect preached. From all sides we learn that the State election was peaceable. There was every evidence at first of John McEnery's election, and that he should have asked the President to suspend recognition of both governments until there could be laid before him all the facts, seems to us based upon far more sense of justice than Attorney General Williams's immediate recognition of Pinchback, who, with a roving commission from nobody, but supported by federal bayonets, now legislates headlong out of office whatever Senator or Assemblyman incurs his dread displeasure.

* * * * * * * *

We do not believe, nor do the committee believe, that the President desires to tyrannize over the South. * * General Grant asks for peace, and we contend that a peaceable union is utterly impossible so long as there is usurpation in any part of the country. Northern Republicans disbelieve in the sincerity of Southern Unionists, and hence are ready to support carpet-baggers. We assure them that no disbelief ever had less foundation in fact, that no people were ever more ready to accept the situation; but that the best way to foster hatred and revolution is to carry out the guerrilla warfare of adventurers like Pinchback. It is quite possible for a negro or a northern man to be a rascal. It is quite possible for a southern man to be honest. Let honesty prevail, and good government will ensue. Let Congress demand a thorough investigation, appointing investigators without fear and without reproach, and Louisiana will be satisfied. Her best people are not so much averse to Kellogg as they fear his Legislature. Let the election records be closely scanned. Attorney General Williams admits that there may have been "irregularities in the registration and election." "Irregularities" is a mild term for tampering with the ballot-box, the ægis of our liberty, and comes with rare grace from the Attorney General of the United States; but the admission is alone sufficient for action, and if upon reassembling Congress does not hearken to the voice of press and people, we shall believe that there are things far more rotten here than in Denmark.

www.ingramcontent.com/pod-product-compliance
Lightning Source LLC
LaVergne TN
LVHW020741120826
845150LV00010B/2289

* 9 7 8 1 4 1 8 1 9 3 9 1 1 *